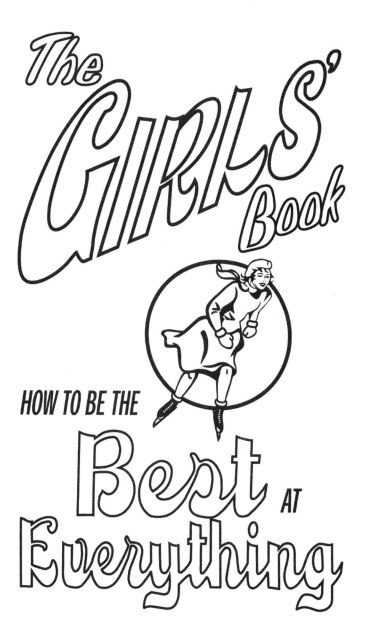

The GIRLS' Book

HOW TO BE THE Best AT Everything

Written by Juliana Foster
Illustrated by Amanda Enright
Edited by Philippa Wingate
Designed by Zoe Quayle

With thanks to Ellen Bailey,
Liz Scoggins, Jo Rooke, and Chris Maynard

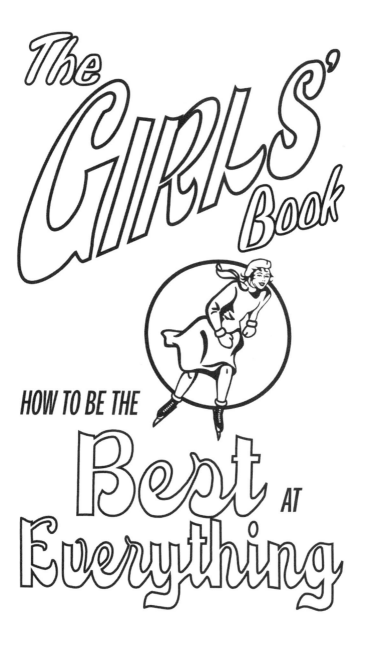

The GIRLS' Book

HOW TO BE THE Best AT Everything

SCHOLASTIC INC.

New York   Toronto   London   Auckland   Sydney
Mexico City   New Delhi   Hong Kong   Buenos Aires

Library of Congress Cataloging-in-Publication data is available.

ISBN 13: 978-0-545-01629-2
ISBN 10: 0-545-01629-0

First published in Great Britain in 2007 by Buster Books, an imprint of Michael O'Mara Books Limited.

Text copyright © Buster Books 2007
Illustrations copyright © Buster Books 2007
Cover design by Angie Allison
Cover illustration by Getty Images

12 11 10 9 8 7 6 5 4 3 2   7 8 9 10 11 12/0

Printed in the U.S.A.
First American edition, September 2007

CONTENTS

NOTE TO READERS

To be the best at everything you'll need to use your
best common sense at all times: Always wear
appropriate safety gear, stay within the law and
local rules, don't hesitate to ask an adult for
assistance, and be considerate of other people.

Beat the rest. Be the best.

HOW TO EXPLAIN WHY YOU ARE LATE FOR SCHOOL

It's always a good idea to have a few excuses up your sleeve should you ever be late for school (through no fault of your own, of course).

"I came all the way to school before I realized I still had my pajamas on, and had to go home and change."

"When I got here my teacher wasn't in the classroom, so I went out looking for her."

"I was abducted by aliens for experimental purposes. I have been gone for 50 years, but fortunately in Earth time it was only an hour."

"I invented a time machine that took me forward to my college graduation. I saw that I will graduate *magna cum laude*, so I think I can take things easy from now on."

"I was helping Little Bo Peep find her sheep."

"I squeezed the toothpaste too hard, and spent all morning getting it back in the tube."

"My parents lost the keys to my cage."

"I'm afraid I can't tell you why I'm late. The government has sworn me to secrecy."

"I'm not late — everyone else is early."

HOW TO LOOK YOUR BEST IN PHOTOS

Do you have photographs of yourself that you'd rather die than let anyone else see? Follow the simple tips below to look fabulous in every picture.

- Don't pose too much. The more natural you look, the better the photo.

- Stand straight with your head held high. Turn your body slightly to the side by putting one leg in front of the other, as shown below. This allows you to show your face and body in a semi-profile, which is very flattering.

- Smile — nobody looks good when they are miserable. You've probably been told to say "cheese," but this can make a smile look more like a grimace. For a natural, gentle smile that is easy to maintain, push your tongue against the back of your top teeth.

- Open your eyes wide (not too wide or you'll look startled or slightly crazy). Don't stare directly at the camera, as this may result in your eyes looking red in the photograph.

- Direct your gaze at a spot just slightly above the camera.

- Relax as much as you can. Just before the photograph is taken, take a deep breath and then let it out.

HOW TO MAKE A TIME CAPSULE

Let future generations know all about you and the world you live in. Find a container that can be sealed to protect its contents. A plastic storage container is ideal. Write, "Not to be opened until the year 2020," or whatever date you like, on the outside. Here are some things to put in the capsule:

- A letter or a recording addressed to the person who finds your capsule. State today's date and tell them a bit about yourself and your life. You could describe what you imagine the future will be like.

- Some photographs of your family and a chart showing your family tree (see pages 48 and 49).

- This week's issue of your favorite magazine.

- A CD of your favorite songs.

- A shiny new coin minted this year.

- Don't include anything valuable or edible.

When the container is full, bury it or put it in your attic.

HOW TO HOST
THE BEST SLEEPOVER

Follow these tips and you'll soon be known for hosting the best sleepovers in town.

• Invite a maximum of four guests, as you want to make sure you have time to give each of them your full attention. Send out handmade invitations well ahead of time so that you can be sure your friends will be free that night. Ask your guests to reply so you know how many are coming.

• It's a good idea to choose a theme for your sleepover and ask each guest to bring one thing that will contribute to the fun. If you're planning a night of salon-style pampering, for example, they could bring nail polish and makeup. Plan activities and decorate your room around the theme.

• Think of some games you can play and gather everything you need to play them before your guests arrive. Get your friends to bring their favorite CDs, DVDs, or board games.

• Be a good hostess — check that everyone has everything they need and knows where the bathroom is. Make sure everyone has somewhere comfortable to sleep (you can ask your guests to bring sleeping bags if necessary).

• Provide plenty of food for your pals, including treats for a midnight snack and breakfast.

• Make sure everyone sticks to the sacred sleepover rule — secrets told at the sleepover stay at the sleepover.

HOW TO TRAIN A DOG
TO SHAKE HANDS

Anyone can teach their dog to sit or come to them, but shaking hands shows the world that you and your dog are pedigree pals.

You can start training your dog when he is about 12 weeks old. Always be consistent and patient when training. You should always be firm and authoritative, but never shout at or hit your dog.

1. Get your dog to sit down in front of you. Praise him when he obeys and offer him a tasty treat.

2. Gently pick up one of his front paws and hold it loosely in your hand, saying, "Shake" as you do so.

3. Reward your dog immediately with a treat and repeat this exercise several times.

4. Next put your hand out and give the command "Shake." Give your dog the chance to put his paw on your open palm as you repeat the command. If he doesn't do it after a couple of seconds, pick up his paw while saying, "Shake."

5. Keep at it — he will figure it out eventually.

HOW TO MAKE SHADOW PUPPETS

Stun your friends and family with these amazing hand shadows.

To achieve the maximum "Wow!" effect, perform your shadow-puppet show in a darkened room with a white or light-colored wall. Aim a powerful desk lamp at the wall and position your hands in front of it. You could even get a friend in on the act.

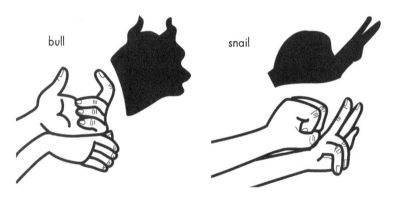

bull   snail

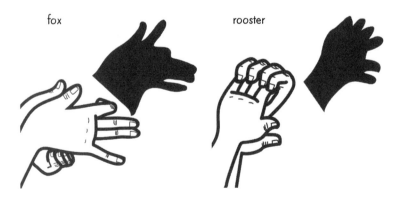

fox   rooster

elephant

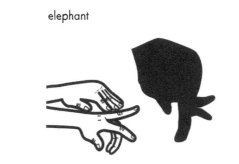

cat

spider

swan

HOW TO MAKE SURE YOUR SNEAKERS SMELL REALLY GOOD

Here are some foolproof ways to avoid those embarrassing moments when you sit back, kick off your shoes, and your friends kick up a fuss. These techniques are guaranteed to ensure you have the sweetest-smelling sneakers around.

- Stuff several unused tea bags into each shoe and leave them there for a couple of days.

- Sprinkle the inside of each shoe with talcum powder.

- Drip a couple of drops of essential oil on the inner soles. Try tea tree, rose, or peppermint oil.

- Fill two clean socks with cat litter (ideally some that your cat hasn't already used), and leave them in your sneakers overnight.

- Tuck fabric softener sheets into the bottom of your shoes, underneath the inner soles.

HOW TO SAVE THE PLANET

Here are some really simple but effective things you can do to help save the planet from the destruction caused by pollution, greenhouse gases, and global warming.

- Make sure all the lights in your house have energy-saving bulbs. Always turn off any lights that aren't needed.

- Turn off or unplug your game console, TV, DVD player, and stereo completely when you are not using them. If the red standby light is on, the appliance is still using electricity.

- Make sure your family recycles everything possible. Newspapers, glass, cans, old clothing, cardboard, plastic containers, and paper should all be recycled.

- Don't throw away toys, books, or CDs that you don't want anymore. Donate them to a local charity.

- Reuse things whenever possible. For example, take along old plastic bags or a canvas tote the next time you go to the supermarket. Tea lights in old jars make magical lights for the garden when you are hosting a barbecue.

- Save water. Turn off the faucet while brushing your teeth. Fill a glass with water to rinse your mouth. Don't run the faucet to rinse plates when you do the dishes. Use a basin of clean water instead. Get your parents to buy a water bucket for the backyard so you can collect rainwater. Use this to water the plants instead of a hose.

- If you feel cold, put on an extra layer of clothing — don't turn up the heat.

HOW TO MAKE A KITE

Kite flying is the perfect activity for a windy day.

1. Make the body of the kite using two double pages from the middle of a tabloid-size newspaper. Join the bottom of one double-sheet to the top of the other with tape to make a large rectangle.

2. To shape your kite, use a ruler to measure 7 inches in from each of the four corners, and mark the correct distances with a pencil. Join up the marks as shown in the drawing below. Use a pair of scissors to cut along the lines.

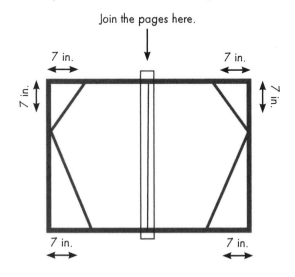

Join the pages here.

7 in.   7 in.

7 in.   7 in.

7 in.   7 in.

3. You need to strengthen your kite with tape. Tape along all the edges of the kite and across it horizontally and vertically, as shown in this drawing.

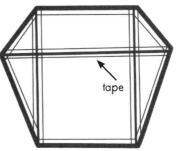

tape

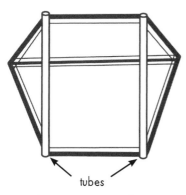

tubes

4. Take two more double pages of the newspaper and make two tight tubes — start at one corner and roll them up diagonally until you reach the other corner. Tape the tubes onto the kite as shown here.

5. Take 60 inches of string and tape one end to the left-hand top corner of the kite, and the other end to the right-hand corner. Tie a piece of string 66 feet long to the middle of this string to make your fly line.

6. Take another piece of string 60 inches long and tape it across the two bottom edges of your kite. The tail is attached to this string. You can make a tail from colored paper or ribbons.

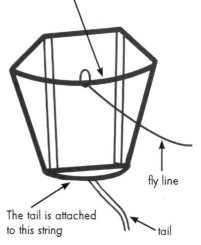

The fly line is attached to this string.

fly line

The tail is attached to this string

tail

11

HOW TO WRITE AN
AWARD-WINNING HAIKU

Haiku is the name given to a type of poem from Japan. The word comes from the Japanese *haikai no ku,* meaning "light verse."

Haikus always have three lines. The first line of a haiku has five syllables. Words are broken up into one or more sound chunks, called syllables. For example, the word *cat* has one syllable, but *croc–o-dile* has three. The first line of a haiku usually introduces the subject of the poem (what the haiku is about). The second line has seven syllables and often describes what the subject of the haiku is doing. The final line has five syllables and acts as a kind of punch line.

Here are two examples:

Sunlight on water
Dapples the riverbed where
Hides the spotted trout.

Black-and-white magpie
Bounces through broken branches,
Hungry for baubles.

HOW TO CUSTOMIZE A T-SHIRT

Before you throw out that boring old T-shirt you never wear anymore, try reinventing it with one of these techniques.

• Make stencils by cutting shapes or letters out of the cardboard from an old cereal box. Tape the stencil to the T-shirt and paint over it with fabric paint. Let the paint dry completely before removing the stencil. For a different look, you can dribble or flick the paint over the stencil instead.

• Try customizing a T-shirt with buttons of all different shapes, sizes, and colors. Start by arranging the buttons — move them around to see what pattern works best. A thick band of buttons around the neckline looks good. Then sew them onto the T-shirt with a needle and thread, or cheat by gluing them on with fabric glue.

• Use scraps of material to make pictures or patterns on the front or back of your T-shirt. Use fabric glue to stick them on. If you add some fabric paint to the edges of the scraps of material, it will help seal them onto the T-shirt.

• Tie-dye a T-shirt your favorite color. Tie-dyeing is a seriously messy business, so work outside if at all possible. Wear rubber gloves and old clothes in case you splash yourself (dye, needless to say, is hard to get off).

For the best tie-dye results, choose a T-shirt that is 100 percent cotton. Mix a packet of powdered clothes dye with 2½ cups of hot water in a bucket. Add 5 tablespoons of salt. Let the mixture cool to room temperature. Tie a long piece of string tightly around the bottom corner of the

T-shirt, then crumple it up and continue wrapping the string around up to the neckline. Tie a knot in the string to hold it tight. Dip the T-shirt into the dye for 20 minutes, then leave it to dry completely before you untie the string. Rinse your T-shirt well.

• If you've tried everything and your T-shirt is just too old and boring to ever look good, make enough money to buy a new one by using it to polish your neighbors' cars.

HOW TO DEAL WITH BULLIES

Most people have been bullied at some time in their lives. If you're being bullied, it's not your fault — the bully is the one with the problem. However, it's crucial to take action.

Find a teacher, parent, or other adult you trust, and tell them exactly what is happening. They don't necessarily have to get involved or even speak to the bully. Just sharing the problem will make you feel better, and they can support you, advise you, and help you stand up for yourself. Most schools have strict policies on bullying and your teachers will have lots of experience in dealing with the problem.

Practice looking and sounding confident. Bullies are usually cowards who pick on people that they think are weaker than themselves. Stand up tall and hold your head up high when you walk around school. Speak in a clear, strong voice and look people directly in the eye.

Whenever possible, ignore any behavior that is intended to make you feel scared or bad about yourself. Convince the bully that you are not bothered by them or hurt by their words — they'll quickly get bored and leave you alone.

Try to think of ways to deal with difficult situations before they occur. Practice things that you could say to someone taunting you. Crying or shouting usually only makes things worse, whereas a clever, casual remark, which is neither rude nor sarcastic, will make you seem confident and in control. Always try to remain calm and be reasonable.

Bullies won't pick on someone who is surrounded by supportive friends. Keep an eye out for the people who often seem to be alone and make an effort to get to know them. This way you'll make lots of new friends and keep the bullies at bay.

No one deserves to be bullied. Don't give in to a bully, don't encourage a bully, and never, ever be a bully yourself.

HOW TO MAKE A FROG
TAKE THE LONG JUMP

Follow this origami project and you will end up with a frog
that, with practice, can be made to leap 6 feet away or
about 2 feet high. Get
your friends to make
one, too, and have a
competition to prove
you are the best.

1. Cut a rectangle
3 x 2 inches out of the
cardboard from an
old cereal box.

2. Fold and unfold corner A
diagonally to D, and then B
diagonally to C, forming a
cross that takes up two-thirds
of the rectangle.

3. Next fold and unfold the
card along the line marked
E and F, as shown.

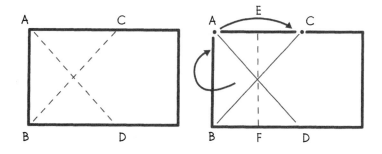

4. Push down the center point where the three folds meet. The card should pop inside out.

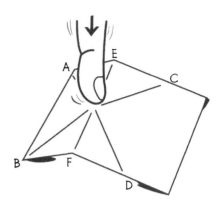

5. Refold all the creases, push points E and F inward, and then fold the top (A/B) across to points C and D.

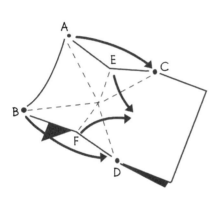

6. Your card should end up looking like this. Fold up corners A and B, as shown here.

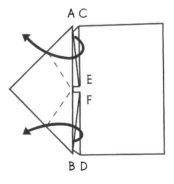

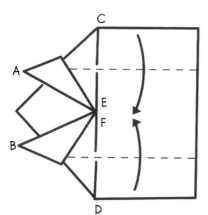

7. Fold in points C and D, as shown here.

8. Make a Z-shaped pleat (this means a gentle crease, not a hard fold) by creasing halfway along the frog's body and then again a quarter of the way along its body.

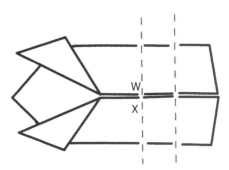

9. To make your frog jump, press down on its back edge, then slide your finger off really quickly, so the frog flicks up into the air.

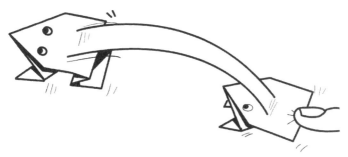

HOW TO GROW YOUR OWN TOMATOES

People say food always tastes better when you have grown it yourself. Try growing some delicious cherry tomatoes. The best time of year to grow tomatoes is toward the end of April when winter is over.

1. You can buy cherry tomato seeds in packets. Alternatively, scoop some seeds out of a cherry tomato you are eating. Rinse them in water and leave them to dry.

2. Fill empty yogurt cups with some potting soil. Push a tomato seed into the center of each cup just below the surface of the soil and cover it. Water the soil lightly.

3. Place your cups on a sunny windowsill. Check them every day, watering as needed so that the soil always feels moist when you touch it with your fingers. Make sure you don't overwater it. After about a week, you should see a tiny shoot appear.

4. After about four weeks, the shoots will have grown into tiny plants. Lift them out of the cups gently, taking as many roots as possible and taking care not to damage them. Transfer them to large flowerpots full of soil, gently patting them into position.

5. Keep checking and watering your tomato plants. After a few weeks, you should see some flowers appearing. Move the plants outside. These flowers will eventually fall off, leaving tiny green tomatoes.

6. When your tomatoes are bright red and feel slightly squishy, they are ripe and ready to pick and eat.

HOW TO TRAVEL WITH JUST ONE BAG

The most sophisticated travelers never struggle with loads of bags. Clever packing is the secret to being one of those glamorous girls who breeze through airports with just one stylish piece of luggage.

First find the right bag. It should be small enough to be allowed onto planes as carry-on luggage (good luggage shops will know the dimensions), light, easy to carry, and distinctive.

Write a list of everything you are going to need, then look over it and ask yourself if there is anything you could possibly live without. Collect each absolutely necessary item and put it on your bed, crossing it off the list as you do so. Take the list with you so that you can make sure you haven't forgotten anything when it's time to return home.

Choose outfits that you can mix and match. Wrap your clothes around other items you're taking. Start with the clothes least likely to crease and work outward.

Pour toiletries into small bottles and place anything that could leak in a plastic bag.

Pack your underwear in your shoes — this saves space and keeps your shoes from getting squashed.

Neatly fold the rest of your clothes and pack them into your suitcase, then fill any gaps with socks.

Wear your bulkiest items of clothing on the trip.

HOW TO DO THE PERFECT HANDSTAND

1. Find an area where the ground is flat and even, and where there is no furniture or other obstacles that could hurt you if you topple over. Grassy areas are good because the ground is softer.

2. Stand up straight and raise your arms above your head.

3. Swing your arms down toward the ground in front of you, bending your upper body as you do so.

4. When your hands touch the ground, you need to move your weight from your feet to your hands. Kick your feet upward, one after the other. This is the trickiest part of the handstand — if you don't kick your legs up high enough, they'll fall back down to the ground, and if you kick them up too hard, you'll flip over.

If you're finding it hard to get your legs to stay up, practice against a wall, or get a friend to catch your calves to steady you as you come up into the handstand.

5. Shift around on your hands a bit until you are nicely balanced. To help at first, keep your knees bent so that your feet hang over your head. Once you've practiced this, try to straighten your legs as much as possible.

HOW TO ACT LIKE A CELEBRITY

Create an aura of mystery and celebrity around yourself by acting like the hottest A-lister in town.

- Buy a pair of enormous sunglasses and wear them all the time, even at night and when you are indoors.

- Say things like "No photographs, please," and "I just wish my fans would leave me alone. I need 'me' time."

- Always look immaculately groomed, even if you are just going to the supermarket.

- Get yourself an entourage to follow you everywhere (walking a few paces behind you, obviously).

- Always look bored, even if you are having fun.

- Always order something that is not on the menu and send it back even when it is delicious.

- Pout a lot.

- Practice signing autographs. Your signature should be flamboyant and completely unreadable.

- Write a list of unreasonable demands to present to your parents. Include things such as "Every drink I am served must contain exactly six ice cubes — no more, no less."

- Ask your father to wear a chauffeur's hat whenever he drives you somewhere.

- Start writing the first part of your autobiography. It must be published before you are 20 years old.

HOW TO MAKE YOUR OWN LUXURY BUBBLE BATH

Here's a quick and simple way to make some luxurious bubble bath that you can enjoy when treating yourself to a well-deserved pampering session. Alternatively, put some in a pretty glass bottle and give it to your best friend as a present.

1. In a clean bowl, mix together 2 cups of clear or light-colored shampoo, 3 cups of water, and 2 teaspoons of salt. Stir the mixture gently until it thickens slightly.

2. Pour a tiny amount of red food coloring into your mixture and stir again. Keep adding the food coloring until the mixture is a perfect pink color.

3. Add 10 drops of an essential oil for a wonderful scent. Rose, lavender, ylang-ylang, sandalwood, marjoram, myrrh, rosewood, and chamomile have relaxing and luxurious scents.

4. Pour the bubble bath into a bottle and close tightly.

HOW TO CONTROL THE WEATHER

Who is going to believe you when you say that you are so powerful that you can control the weather? Well, show them who's in charge of the elements by creating your own rainbow or a flash of lightning.

Rainbow: All you need is a sunny day, a glass filled with water almost to the brim, and a sheet of white paper.

Place the glass so that it is half on and half off the edge of a table, being careful not to let it slide off. Make sure the sun shines directly through the water onto the floor.

Place the paper on the floor, where a rainbow is formed by the light passing through the glass.

Lightning: Put on a wool sweater. Blow up an ordinary balloon and scout around your house to find a large metal surface (such as a refrigerator door or the side of a filing cabinet).

Turn off the lights to darken the room as much as possible. Rub the balloon against your wool sweater about ten times. Then wave it close to the metal surface. You'll see a flash or spark, like lightning, jump between the balloon and the metal surface.

The lightning effect happens because you have created static electricity on the surface of the balloon that escapes by jumping toward the metal surface.

HOW TO MAKE
A FRIENDSHIP BRACELET

These make great gifts to swap with your friends. Start by practicing with four or five strands of yarn or embroidery thread. Once you've got the hang of it, you can use as many different threads as you like to make really colorful, chunky bracelets.

1. Choose four strands of yarn or embroidery thread in different colors, each about 24 inches long. Bind them together with a knot at the top. Tape the knotted end to something to secure the bracelet while you work — try the back of a chair.

2. Take the first thread on the left (thread A) and wrap it over and around thread B to make a knot, as shown above. Hold thread B so that it is taut when you do this and make sure the knot is tight. Repeat this to make a double knot.

3. Still using thread A, make a double knot around thread C, and then finally around D. When you have completed the first row, thread A will be on the right and thread B (the next thread you will be working with) will be on the left.

4. Repeat steps two and three with thread B, then C, and then D. Then start with A again. When your bracelet is long enough to go around your wrist, tie the ends together in another firm knot. To wear it, tie the two knotted ends together around your wrist.

HOW TO IMPROVE YOUR MEMORY

The best way to improve your memory is to exercise your brain. Try doing a few puzzles every day — newspapers usually have a daily puzzle page, or you can buy different kinds of puzzle books.

Learning skills is a great way to whip your brain into shape. Try mastering something new, like learning how to play a musical instrument or learning how to knit.

Brush up on your observational skills. Ask someone to collect 15 small objects from around the house and place them in front of you on a tray. Study them for 30 seconds, then leave the room and try to write down all the objects you remember. Or get your friend to remove one object while you cover your eyes. Guess which object is missing from the tray.

One of the easiest ways to remember things is by repetition. The more you practice, the faster you will memorize things. Try learning a new poem every week. Read it out loud to yourself a few times until you can recite it by heart.

Mnemonics, which are memory tools, are handy as well. The trick is to associate the information you need to remember with simple sentences. For example, you could use the name "ROY G. BIV" to recall the colors that appear in the rainbow, and their order (Red, Orange, Yellow, Green, Blue, Indigo, Violet).

Rhymes are useful for remembering information, too. Here's one to help you remember how many days there are in each month.

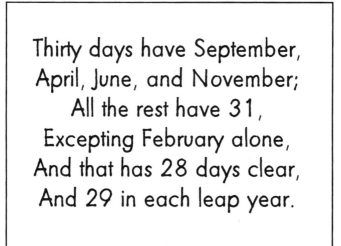

Thirty days have September,
April, June, and November;
All the rest have 31,
Excepting February alone,
And that has 28 days clear,
And 29 in each leap year.

HOW TO BLOW THE BIGGEST BUBBLE-GUM BUBBLE

Put a piece of bubble gum in your mouth and chew it well. The larger the piece of gum, the larger the bubble you can blow. Make sure it is soft and stretchy.

With your tongue, flatten the bubble gum across the backs of your top and bottom front teeth.

Using your tongue again, push the center of the gum out between your teeth. Seal your lips all around the bulge in the gum. Finally, blow into the bulge of bubble gum, and see how big you can get your bubble before it pops and sticks all over your face and hair!

HOW TO SURVIVE IN A HORROR MOVIE

- When it appears that you have killed a monster, never approach it to check if it's really dead — it will pounce on you.

- When running away from a monster, expect to fall over at least twice.

- Never accept invitations from strangers who live in isolated areas and have no contact with society.

- If your car breaks down at night, don't go to a deserted-looking mansion to phone for help.

- Do not search the basement — especially if the lights have just gone out and the phone is dead.
  - If your date has fangs, go home.
- If your date has rotting green flesh and behaves more like a zombie than most dates, go home.
  - Never, ever say, "I'll be right back." You won't be.

HOW TO WHISTLE REALLY LOUDLY

A wolf whistle is a really good way to get someone's attention — or to really annoy them.

1. Wash your hands. Place the tips of your thumb and index finger together to form an O shape.

2. Put these fingers into your mouth as far as the first joint. Point the nails of these fingers toward the middle of your tongue.

3. Close and tighten your lips around your fingers, so that air can only escape through the gap between them.

4. Press your tongue against the back of your bottom teeth.

5. Breathe out steadily, using your tongue to direct the air through the gap between your fingers. Pull down with your fingers pressing on your bottom lip.

6. Keep practicing, moving your fingers, lips, and tongue just a tiny bit at a time until you hear a whistle.

HOW TO BE A NATURAL BEAUTY

You can use ingredients you'll find in the fridge and kitchen cupboards to get fresh and healthy-looking skin and hair.

• **Exfoliate:** Mix together 1 tablespoon of plain yogurt, 1 drizzle of honey, and 1 teaspoon of granulated sugar. Rub the mixture gently over your face to exfoliate (get rid of dead skin) and leave your skin glowing. Rinse well.

• **Face mask:** If you have dry skin, mash up a quarter of an avocado with 2 tablespoons of honey. Spread it over your face (avoiding your eyes) and leave for about 15 minutes before rinsing with warm water.

• **Eyes:** To get rid of dark circles around your eyes, cut a fresh fig in half and place the halves over your eyes for 15 minutes, while lying on your bed and relaxing. For tired eyes, enjoy the cooling effect of two slices of cucumber placed over your eyes. To soothe your eyes, soak cotton pads in rose water, milk, or aloe vera juice and place over your lids.

• **Condition:** For smooth, silky hair, beat an egg yolk in a bowl, then mix in a teaspoon of olive oil, drip by drip. Add a cup of warm water. After shampooing, spread the mixture evenly over your hair and leave for a few minutes before rinsing it off.

Tip: Don't use any foods that you are allergic to.

HOW TO MAKE A STAINED-GLASS WINDOW

Follow these instructions to make a beautiful "stained-glass" window.

1. Take two pieces of black cardboard and two pieces of waxed paper, all of equal size. Decide on a simple picture, for example, a leaf or a dolphin. Sketch your shape onto one piece of cardboard.

2. Hold the two pieces of cardboard neatly together and cut out your shape, leaving a border of cardboard around it.

3. Select wax crayons in the colors you want to decorate your picture. With a sharp craft knife, carefully shave the crayons.

4. Spread the wax shavings on one of the sheets of waxed paper. Place the other sheet on top and run a warm iron over them.

Tip: Ask an adult before using the iron!

wax shavings   waxed paper

34

5. To assemble the window, place one piece of the cardboard flat on a table and glue the sandwich of waxed paper to it. Then glue the other piece of cardboard on top, trapping the waxed paper between the two pieces of board. Hang your finished work near a window so that the light shines through it.

HOW TO EXECUTE A SPECTACULAR HIGH DIVE

Prepare:

Climb up to the high board at your local pool. At the top, stand up straight with your hands by your sides and walk toward the end of the board. As you reach the edge, turn around and stand with your back to the water.

It is essential to look completely calm and confident. Do NOT shake as if you are terrified that it is such a long way down.

Rise onto the balls of your feet, and take tiny steps backward until your heels are over the end of the board and your toes are on the very edge.

Launch: Stretch your arms above your head, with your thumbs touching. Then bend your knees, drop your arms down by your sides, and push down on the board. Jump up and away from the end of the board, swinging your arms forward, upward, and over your head as you jump.

Pike: As you rise, lift your legs so they are pointing straight up. Start bending your body forward at the waist until you are folded in half. Reach your fingers toward your toes.

pike

Layout: Immediately start to straighten out your body. Your head should now be pointing toward the water. Bring your arms and hands forward so they are stretched above your head.

entrance

Entrance: As you enter the water, your body must be completely straight, so that you make a minimal splash.

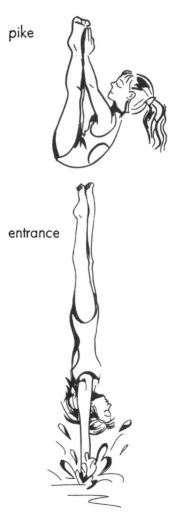

HOW TO MAKE SUGAR MICE

Sugar mice are delicious and very easy to make. If you don't eat them all yourself, put some in a decorated box and give them to a friend.

1. In a bowl, mix 2 level teaspoons of powdered egg white and 2 tablespoons of warm water.

2. Hold a sifter over the bowl, pour in about 1 pound of confectioners' sugar, sift it, and mix it in. Add drops of lemon juice until the mixture is soft and spongy.

3. Put a small amount of the mixture into another bowl and add some red food coloring, drop by drop, until the mixture turns pink. You'll use this to make the ears.

4. Take lumps of the white mixture and roll and knead them into the shape of mice.

5. Use tiny amounts of the pink mixture to make ears. Edible silver balls (purchased at a baking supply store) pushed into the icing make great noses and eyes, and you can use strings of black licorice to make tails.

6. Place your mice on a baking tray in a cool spot and leave them to set for a couple of hours.

HOW TO MAKE SENSE
WHILE TALKING NONSENSE

Oxymoron is the name given to a figure of speech where two words or phrases that seem to contradict each other are put together. Oxymorons don't make any sense, yet they make complete sense, and are ideal for baffling your friends. Here are some to use:

- Pretty ugly • Deafening silence
- Constant change • Exact estimate • Instant classic
- Liquid gas • Advanced beginner • Alone together

HOW TO SPOT A GENIUS

Ask a friend to count the number of F's in the following text.

FINISHED FILES ARE THE
RESULT OF YEARS OF SCIENTIFIC
STUDY COMBINED WITH THE
EXPERIENCE OF YEARS.

There are six F's in the sentence, but most people only count three. This is because many people's brains don't register that the word *of* contains an F.

Anyone who counts all six F's on the first try is a genius.

HOW TO BE A MATH MASTER

Ask your friends to try this simple addition problem. Read it out loud just as it appears below. Don't let your friends use a pencil and paper or a calculator — they must figure it out in their heads.

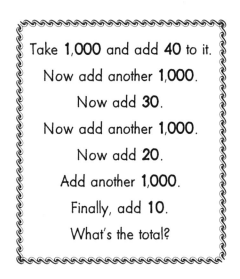

Take **1,000** and add **40** to it.

Now add another **1,000**.

Now add **30**.

Now add another **1,000**.

Now add **20**.

Add another **1,000**.

Finally, add **10**.

What's the total?

Your friends will probably say the answer is 5,000.

Congratulations, you are a math magician, because this is the wrong answer. The right answer is 4,100.

If your friends don't believe you, make them do the problem again using a calculator as you read the instructions aloud.

HOW TO MAKE A BIRD FEEDER

In the winter months it's hard for birds to find food. Give them a helping hand by hanging this easy-to-make feeder from a tree or balcony, and watch a dazzling variety of birds flock to your backyard.

Find a large, dry pinecone that has opened up, rinse it under a faucet, and leave it to dry. When it's dry, spread peanut butter all over the cone with a spoon, making sure you fill all the crevices.

Spread some birdseed on a paper plate and roll the pinecone around in it. Press down quite hard so that the seeds stick to the peanut butter and don't fall off. Make sure all the peanut butter is covered with seeds.

Tie a long length of string to the stalk of the cone and hang it out of the reach of greedy cats and squirrels.

HOW TO MAKE A POM-POM

Pom-poms are incredibly easy to make and you can use them to decorate many things. Customize your clothes by sewing them on scarves and wool hats, or even hang them on the Christmas tree. Yarn comes in a huge variety of colors and textures, so get creative. . . .

You'll need yarn, a pair of scissors, and a piece of stiff cardboard to make the pompom template.

1. Draw two identical circles on the cardboard (try tracing around a circular object, such as a can). The bigger the circles, the larger your pom-pom will be. Draw a smaller circle inside each of the large circles. Cut out the large circles, and then cut out the inner circles, so that you have two ring-shaped pieces of cardboard.

2. Take the yarn you want to use and cut it into 3⅓ foot lengths.

3. Lay the two rings on top of each other, trapping one end of the yarn between the two pieces of cardboard. Feed the other end of the yarn across the ring and through the hole.

4. When you have used up the yarn, start wrapping a new piece. You don't need to tie it to the last one — just make sure that the end of it is lined up with the outer edge of the rings.

5. Keep wrapping until the hole is so tiny you can't get the yarn through.

6. Slip the blades of your scissors through the yarn and between the two pieces of cardboard. Cut the yarn all around the outside edge of the rings.

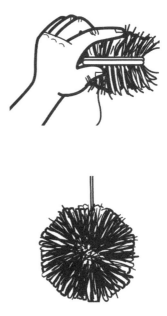

7. Take another length of yarn and slip it between the two rings. Tie it in a firm knot around the yarn that passes through the hole in the rings. Slip the cardboard rings off and fluff up your pom-pom.

HOW TO WIN A STARING CONTEST

Stand facing a friend and stare into each other's eyes. The first person to blink or look away loses the contest. It's not as easy as it sounds. Your eyes dry out if you don't blink, and they start to sting. Follow these tips to be unbeatable.

• Before the contest starts, close your eyes as tightly as you can, and for as long as you can, to produce tears that will keep your eyes moist.

• Open your eyes wide during the contest and, when you think you are about to blink, open them even wider. This goes against your natural instincts, but will actually make your eyes water, thus keeping them moist.

• When you are about to blink, squint and furrow your brow. Again, this will produce tears and help you to stare longer.

HOW TO TURN WATER INTO LEMONADE

Gather your friends and tell them you are about to perform a miracle — you'll turn dull tap water into delicious lemonade.

To make sure you succeed, you need to prepare a "trick" jug beforehand and maybe have a few practice runs.

1. Get hold of a large jug that is made of china or pottery. It must not be see-through or you will give the trick away.

2. Attach a bit of sticky putty to the bottom of a plastic cup and put it inside the jug, pressing it down hard so that it stays firmly in place.

3. Tightly pack small sponges or absorbent rags around the plastic cup so they don't fall out when the jug is tipped.

4. Carefully fill the cup inside the jug with lemonade.

5. Now you are ready to perform the miracle. Gather your audience and seat them so they can't see inside the jug.

6. Fill a glass with water. Pour some into the jug, making sure the water doesn't go into the plastic cup, but onto the rags and sponges around the cup, where it will be absorbed.

7. Mutter some impressive-sounding magic words and wave your hands mysteriously over the jug.

8. Tip the jug and pour the contents of the plastic cup into an empty glass. Offer the glass of lemonade to a member of your audience to taste. Sit back and accept your applause.

HOW TO CONVINCE PEOPLE YOU ARE AN ANIMAL EXPERT

Here are some facts that, when casually dropped into the conversation, will convince your friends that you are a world authority on the animal kingdom.

Introduce these facts with phrases such as "My sources indicate that . . ." or "My research has shown that . . ." or "I feel sure that my colleagues would not dispute that . . .":

. . . cats have 32 muscles in each ear.

. . . crocodiles can't stick their tongues out.

. . . a duck's quack doesn't echo.

. . . all polar bears are left-handed.

. . . cows can walk up stairs, but not down them.

. . . a snail can sleep for three years.

. . . the longest recorded flight of a chicken is 13 seconds.

. . . ants don't sleep.

. . . a hedgehog's heart beats an average of 300 times a minute.

. . . a donkey can see all four of its feet at the same time.

. . . a mole can dig a tunnel 295 feet long in one night.

. . . an ostrich's eye is bigger than its brain.

. . . butterflies taste with their feet.

. . . if you cut off a cockroach's head, it can survive for weeks before it starves to death.

. . . dolphins sleep with one eye open.

. . . slugs have four noses.

. . . giraffes can clean their ears with their tongues.

. . . sharks don't have bones.

. . . kangaroos can't walk backward.

HOW TO DO A QUICK CARD TRICK

Shuffle a deck of cards. Peek at the bottom card and remember it. Ask your friend to pick any card, memorize it, but not show you. Cut the deck. Hold out the top half of the deck and ask your friend to put their card on top of it. Place the bottom half of the deck on top of the top half. Tap the deck mysteriously. Then turn over the cards, one by one. When you come to the card you saw at the bottom of the pack, you'll know your friend's card is the next card.

HOW TO MAKE A CHART SHOWING YOUR FAMILY TREE

Charting the history of your family is fascinating. Ask your relatives to help you find out all the names and personalities of the past.

It's best to work backward when you are writing out a family tree. So start by writing your name at the bottom of a large piece of paper.

Write the names of all your brothers and sisters, in order of age, on the same line as your name. The oldest should be on the left and the youngest on the right.

With a ruler, draw a short vertical line above each of the names. Join the top of these lines together with a long horizontal line.

Next draw a single vertical line upward from the middle of the horizontal line that connects you and your brothers and sisters.

At the top of this vertical line, draw a short horizontal to make a T-shape, and write your dad's name to the left of the line and your mom's name to the right of it.

Next put the names of your mom's brothers and sisters to the right of her name, and put the names of your dad's brothers and sisters to the left of his name. Remember to put the oldest on the left and the youngest on the right.

Using the same method you did for your brothers and sisters, join up the names of the brothers and sisters in your

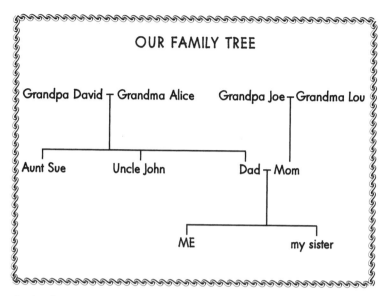

OUR FAMILY TREE

Grandpa David ⊤ Grandma Alice   Grandpa Joe ⊤ Grandma Lou

Aunt Sue   Uncle John   Dad ⊤ Mom

ME   my sister

dad's family, and draw a vertical line to the names of their parents (your grandparents). Do the same for your mom's side of the family.

Write the names of your grandparents and their brothers and sisters, and connect them to the names of their parents (your great-grandparents).

Keep going in this manner until you have traced your family tree as far back as anyone can remember.

Tip: You could add the birth dates for some of the people on the chart if you can find them out, and birth and death dates for those who are no longer alive.

HOW TO ANNOY PEOPLE IN AN ELEVATOR

- Grin at another passenger and then announce, "I've got new socks on."

- Crash from side to side as if you're sailing in rough seas.

- Suggest you all join in a sing-along.

- Say, "Ding!" at each floor.

- Salute and say, "Welcome aboard," every time someone gets in.

- Open your bag and, while peering inside, ask, "Got enough air in there?"

- Meow occasionally.

- Stand silent and motionless in the corner, facing the wall, without getting off when the elevator stops.

- Make race-car noises when anyone gets in.

HOW TO GIVE YOURSELF THE PERFECT MANICURE

The perfect manicure is an essential skill to master if you always want to look well groomed and immaculate.

1. Dab some cuticle cream (lip balm or petroleum jelly will do just as well) on your cuticles — these are the strips of skin at the base of your nails. Rub the cuticle cream in. Then soak your fingers in a bowl full of warm, soapy water for ten minutes to soften the skin and nails.

2. Rinse your hands and check that your nails are very clean. If necessary, give them a scrub with a nailbrush or an old toothbrush. Remove any dirt under the nails with a cuticle stick. Dry your hands thoroughly.

3. Very gently, push your cuticles back with the flat end of a cuticle stick. This will make your cuticles look neater and more rounded.

4. After washing and drying your hands again, trim your nails to the length you like them using a fingernail clipper.

5. Next perfect the shape of your nails with a nail file. Make sure you file in one direction only, not back and

forth, as this can weaken the nails and make them split. Give your hands one last wash and dry them.

6. Now it's time to apply some nail polish. Clear polish looks subtle, classy, and often lasts longer than bright colors. To avoid lumps, put your bottle of polish in the fridge for five minutes before using it. This makes it smoother to apply.

To avoid messy streaks, use only three strokes per nail and don't get too much polish on your brush when you dip it. The first stroke should go down the center of the nail. Then do the right and left sides.

Let your nails dry for at least 15 minutes. The longer you resist the temptation to do anything with your hands, the less likely you will be to smudge your beautifully manicured nails.

HOW TO BE AN AUTOGRAPH HUNTER

Buy or make a scrapbook or album for your autograph collection and decorate it however you want.

Regularly check your local paper for events that celebrities will be attending, such as book signings or store openings, and ask someone to take you along. Be prepared to wait in line patiently for an autograph.

If you spot a celebrity out and about and want to approach them for an autograph, always be polite. Approach them only if you feel it is appropriate — nobody likes being interrupted during a meal or in the middle of a phone call, for example.

Look up the addresses of fan clubs or celebrities' agents, and write to them asking for an autograph. If you put some thought into your letter, you will be more likely to get a reply. Tell them why you are a fan and a bit about yourself. Always include a stamped envelope with your address on it and a blank piece of paper for them to sign.

HOW TO FIND YOUR BLIND SPOT

Place one hand over your left eye and hold this book in your right hand. Stare at the black circle below.

Gradually move the book closer and closer to your face, still staring at the circle.

When the book is a certain distance from your face, you will notice that the star will vanish. Bingo! You have found your blind spot.

The blind spot effect is caused by a lack of light-detecting receptor cells on the optic disk of the retina.

●

HOW TO ICE-SKATE

Before you even set foot on an ice rink, make sure you have all the right gear. Ice is a seriously hard surface to fall on, and everyone takes a few tumbles at first. Wear knee and elbow pads and thick gloves to protect yourself.

Make sure that your skates fit well and don't rub your heels or squash your toes.

When you first get on the ice, take some time to get your balance. If possible, go with a friend who already knows how to skate. Get her to hold you steady and pull you around on the ice until you get used to the sensation.

Keep your knees slightly bent at all times to help with your balance — you shouldn't be able to see your toes. Your shoulders should be slightly forward, in line with your knees.

Try to relax your body, especially your knees. This will help your balance; plus, if you fall over, you'll be less likely to hurt yourself. If you do feel you are about to fall backward, try to resist the temptation to put your arms out to stop yourself. A sore bottom is better than a broken wrist!

To skate forward, shift your weight over onto your left foot and push your right foot outward in a diagonal stroke. Then repeat, transferring your weight to your right leg and pushing out with your left foot. Move your body with these strides. When you feel more confident, try to take longer strides. With practice, you will begin to be able to glide across the ice.

The easiest way to stop is to place one foot behind you with the front point of that skate digging into the ice. Drag this back foot along the ice to slow yourself down until you stop.

HOW TO PRESS FLOWERS

Follow these instructions to press your favorite blooms and enjoy colorful summer flowers, leaves, and foliage all year long, without buying a special flower press.

When choosing which flowers to press, think about how a flower will look when it's flat. Some flowers, like daffodils, are oddly shaped and don't look good when flattened.

Stick to flowers with simple shapes and not too many petals (you can always carefully remove a few petals if necessary, to thin a flower head out).

Here's how to achieve the best results when pressing:

1. Pick flowers when they are dry. If they are damp with rain or dew, there's a danger they may get moldy.

2. Choose a big, heavy book, like a phone book or an encyclopedia. Cut sheets of cardboard so they are slightly smaller than the size of a page in the book. Then cut squares of newspaper and tissue paper that are 4 x 4 inches.

3. Place a newspaper square on top of a sheet of cardboard. Then place a square of tissue paper on top of the newspaper. Carefully lay your flowers and leaves on the tissue paper. Make sure they aren't touching one another.

4. Cover the flowers with another layer of tissue paper, then newspaper, then cardboard. Keep making these "flower sandwiches" until all your flowers are laid out. Slot them between different pages of your flower-pressing book.

5. Put your flower-pressing book at the bottom of a stack of books and leave it there for a couple of weeks. When it is time to remove the flowers, do so carefully.

Use your pressed flowers and leaves to make pictures and cards, or decorate the cover of a notebook. Lay them out artistically on the surface you want to decorate, then cover with some laminating sheets.

Tip: Don't pick flowers growing in parks, and ask before you pick flowers from people's gardens.

HOW TO MAKE AN ICY MILK SHAKE WITHOUT A BLENDER (OR ICE CREAM!)

Dying for an icy-cold milk shake, but don't have the proper ingredients? Don't worry! Here's a superspeedy way to make mouthwatering icy milk shakes!

1. Pour a cup of milk into a plastic food bag that can be sealed and add a tablespoon of sugar and a few drops of vanilla extract. Seal the bag tightly and then give it a good shake to mix up the ingredients.

2. Fill a larger plastic bag with ice cubes. Place the bag containing the milk shake mix inside the larger plastic bag and tie a tight knot in the top.

3. Shake the bag for five minutes. Be careful because water will leak out of the bag, so it is a good idea to do this part outside.

4. Remove the small bag, open it carefully, and enjoy.

HOW TO MAKE A CAMP IN THE WILDERNESS

So, your plane has crashed in the middle of nowhere and you need to keep yourself alive until help arrives.

You can survive for much longer without food than without water, so finding water is your first priority. You need to find a spot to set up camp that is near a source of water, but not too near, as wild animals may gather there to drink.

You need to build a lean-to to keep you dry and protected from the sun or rain. Every lean-to requires a strong supporting structure. See if you can find a fallen tree, a natural cave, or a big rock to build your lean-to against. Collect thick sticks and branches and prop them up at an angle along the tree trunk or rock face. Make sure the space under the sticks is long enough to cover your whole body when you lie underneath them.

Gather smaller branches and sticks, and use them to fill the gaps between the larger ones. Then heap leaves, grass, moss, ferns, or whatever you can find over the sticks. This will keep some of the wind and rain out of your lean-to, and hopefully keep some of your body heat inside.

Collect a large stack of dry wood to make a fire. You can also use bark or even dry animal dung. Make your fire at least ten paces from your lean-to, as you don't want the smoke to bother you, or your lean-to to catch fire.

To keep yourself extra warm at night, you could heat rocks on the fire and then bury them in the ground and sleep on top of them.

It is essential to keep your fire lit at all times and have a pile of damp leaves ready beside it. If you hear a plane or helicopter fly overhead, throw the leaves on top of the fire to create a plume of smoke that will attract attention.

When it comes to foraging for food, be careful. Don't be tempted by mushrooms — even experts sometimes find it hard to tell which ones are good to eat and which are poisonous. Berries can also be dangerous. As a general rule, most white or yellow berries are poisonous and most blue or black berries are not, but there are exceptions. Your best bet is to eat insects. It may sound disgusting, but they are nutritious and are not likely to be harmful.

It is better to stay in one place if you know someone will be looking for you.

HOW TO GROOM A HORSE

1. Put a halter on the horse and tie it up with a lead rope so that it doesn't wander off while you're trying to groom it.

2. Start with a currycomb to loosen up any dried-on dirt. Use mostly firm, circular motions, but you'll need a lighter touch on bony or sensitive areas like the legs or belly. Avoid the horse's face.

3. Use a body brush, which has thick, stiff bristles, to remove all the hair and dirt you've just dislodged. Use long sweeps, starting at the neck and sweeping in the direction the hair grows. Again, avoid the face.

4. Gently wipe the horse's eyes and nose with a wet sponge or soft cloth.

5. Use a mane comb to get tangles out of the mane and tail. Start at the base of the strands and comb downward. When you're combing out the tail, don't stand directly behind the horse. Stay slightly to one side to avoid being kicked.

6. Use a soft-bristled brush in sweeping strokes all over the horse to make its coat really shine.

7. Clean out the horse's hooves with a pick to remove any dirt or stones. Start at the heel and work up to the toe, avoiding the sensitive V-shaped area.

HOW TO ANNOY YOUR FAMILY AND FRIENDS

Here are some excellent practical jokes guaranteed to annoy your parents, brothers, sisters, or friends.

• Wait for a rainy day. Pour paper confetti into your mom's closed umbrella and wait for her to go outside and open it.

• Use a pin to prick a hole near the top of your brother's drinking straw.

• Chew on some small white mints, then pretend to bump into a wall. Moan and spit the mints out. Your dad will think you are spitting out your broken teeth.

• Find an old rag. Put a coin on the floor and stand nearby. When your sister tries to pick up the coin, rip the old rag. She'll think she has torn her pants.

• When a friend is drinking a can of soda, wait until they are not looking and pour in some sugar. The sugar will make the drink froth up and pour out of the can.

• Send one of your friends on a "fool's errand" — this means asking her to do something that is meaningless and impossible. For example, ask her to go to the store and buy you some waterproof towels, or some striped paint, or a tin of elbow grease.

HOW TO KEEP
A MESSAGE SECRET

If you master the art of making your own invisible ink and how to make it visible again, you can write secret messages to your friends. Anyone who's not in on the secret will just see a blank piece of paper.

1. First mix equal amounts of water and baking soda in a bowl. A little goes a long way, so you won't need very much of either ingredient.

2. Dip a toothpick or Q-tip into the mixture and write your message on a sheet of paper.

3. To reveal the message, simply hold the paper up to a lightbulb (don't make contact with it or you will singe the paper). You'll see the message appear in brown as the heat produced by the bulb reacts with the baking soda.

4. Another way of revealing the message is to brush some purple grape juice over the paper using a paintbrush. The baking soda and grape juice react together and change the color of the writing.

You are now ready to communicate in complete secrecy.

HOW TO MAKE A FAKE MESS

Freak out your folks with a fake mess!

Decide what kind of mess you want to make — a coffee spill, an ink accident, or how about cat throw-up on your mom's favorite top? Mix up some paint. A milk-chocolate brown works for coffee, royal blue for ink, and pink and orange is good for throw-up. Add drops of white craft glue until the paint is thick and sticky.

If you want to make the fake throw-up super-convincing, you should add some oatmeal to the mixture for extra realism.

Pour the paint mixture onto a piece of waxed paper and leave it to dry completely. Cut around the edges of the paint so none of the waxed paper can be seen.

Place the mess wherever it will have the best effect — on your dad's favorite tie, on the beautifully polished wooden table. Set up some props, like a coffee mug lying on its side nearby. Then simply wait for someone to come along, spot it, and shriek!

HOW TO PREDICT THE WEATHER

A barometer is an instrument that measures changes in atmospheric pressure and can therefore give you an idea of what the weather is going to be like. You can make a simple barometer by following these instructions.

1. Stretch an ordinary balloon by blowing it up and then letting all the air out.

2. Cut the balloon in half. You only need the top half, so throw away the neck of the balloon.

3. Stretch the top of the balloon over an empty glass jar and secure it tightly with a rubber band around the rim.

4. Lay a drinking straw flat on the balloon "lid" so that one end is in the center and the other end hangs off the side. Tape the straw in place, making sure the tape is about a thumb's width from the end of the straw.

5. Place your barometer against a wall and fix a piece of paper to the wall directly behind it. Record the position of the top of the straw with a pencil mark on the paper.

6. You are now ready to predict the weather. There are changes in air pressure just before a change of weather. When it is about to be sunny, high pressure will cause the balloon to be "pushed" downward and the straw will tilt upward. When rain is on the way, low pressure will cause the balloon to be "pushed" upward and the straw will tilt down. The different marks you make on the paper will show how the pressure changes from day to day.

HOW TO MAKE AN EGGHEAD

1. First you need to drain the insides of an egg without breaking the shell. Place the egg in an eggcup. Carefully pierce a small hole in the top of the egg using a needle, then turn the egg upside down and use the needle again to make another hole in the bottom. You will need to gently enlarge this hole by turning the pin around and around.

2. Push the needle into the larger hole. Jiggle it a few times to break up the yolk and the sac. Remove the needle, and gently blow through the small hole so that the contents of the egg come out of the larger hole and into a bowl.

3. Now the inside of the egg needs to be cleaned. Do this by gently placing the egg in a bowl of warm water and liquid soap. Fill up the egg with the warm water and then let it drain out of the larger hole in the bottom. Make sure to rinse the egg thoroughly.

4. With your clean, empty shell, you can begin designing your egg friend. Take the needle again and make two larger holes on either side of the egg where you would like the arms to be. Take a pipe cleaner and gently push it through the hole on one side of the egg and out the hole on the other side of the egg.

5. Use yarn to make some hair. Glue it onto the egg, covering the top hole. To make "feet" for your egghead, cut off the bottom of a toilet paper roll approximately 1 inch from the bottom, paint it black, and stick it onto a circular piece of black cardboard that is slightly wider than your toilet paper roll. Add a face using either markers or paint.

HOW TO WALK THE DOG

This is a yo-yo trick, not a fun outing for one of your canine pals, and is best performed on a wooden or tiled floor.

1. Hold the yo-yo in your hand with your palm facing upward. Slip your middle finger through the loop of the string. Make sure the string winds up from your finger over the top of the yo-yo toward your body, in the direction indicated by the arrow in the top picture.

2. Bend your arm at the elbow, then straighten it. When your arm is almost straight in front of you, flick your wrist, releasing the yo-yo forward and downward. Turn your hand palm down and lower your arm as the yo-yo falls. As the yo-yo reaches the ground, stop lowering your arm and give the string an upward tug. The yo-yo will climb back up the string to your hand. Catch it.

3. This time, repeat steps two and three, but as the yo-yo drops downward, let it touch the ground. It will roll along the floor away from you. This is "walking the dog."

HOW TO SHOW OFF YOUR SUPERHUMAN STRENGTH

Impress your friends by telling them you have the powers of a superhero and can prove it with this trick.

Hold a full-size umbrella horizontally in front of you so that it is level with your shoulders and about 10 inches away from your body. Your elbows should be bent at all times, so that they are almost at right angles.

Get a friend to grab hold of the umbrella near the ends. Make sure that her hands are nearer the ends of the umbrella than yours.

Ask her to try and move you by pushing against the umbrella as hard as she can. As she pushes, push upward to keep the umbrella in position. This deflects the pressure upward rather than against your body and your friend will not be able to budge you.

To make this an even more impressive feat, you can ask another friend to add her weight, by standing behind the first person and pushing against her shoulders. You should be able to resist them both.

HOW TO MAKE A DRUM

A drum is one of the easiest (and one of the noisiest) instruments you can make from everyday objects found around the house.

1. Find an empty tin can. Coffee cans are good to use, as they are slightly larger than other cans.

2. Cut some paper so that it is as tall as the can and long enough to wrap all the way around its side. Decorate one side of the paper using paint, glue, and glitter or anything else you like. Use your imagination.

3. Glue or tape the decorated paper to the can.

4. Place the can on a piece of waxed paper and draw a circle around it about 1 inch larger in diameter than the can. Cut out the circle. Now cut five more circles of exactly the same size. Cover the first paper circle with a thin layer of glue and stick another circle on top of it. Repeat this until all six circles are glued together. This will be the "skin" of your drum. Allow the glue to dry overnight.

5. Place your paper circle over the open end of the can and secure it tightly with a rubber band.

6. You can make some drumsticks with two pencils and two corks. Simply push the sharpened end of the pencil into the cork. Tap your drum with the cork ends.

Different cans will make different sounds, so you can build your own drum kit using cans of various sizes and shapes.

HOW TO FLOAT A FRIEND

This is an amazing trick. There's no real explanation for why or how it works — it just does. Find five friends willing to take part in your experiment. Choose one friend to be the subject who will be lifted, and ask her to sit on a chair.

Ask each of the other four girls to place their hands together, with their palms touching and their fingers outstretched.

One girl must place her fingers under the bent left knee of the subject on the chair. Another places her fingers in the same position under the right knee. The third girl places her fingers under one of the subject's armpits, and the fourth girl places her fingers under the other armpit.

Tell your friends to try to lift the person up from the chair. Chances are they will fail.

Next ask everyone to stack their hands one on top of the other on top of the subject's head and press down lightly. Tell them to keep pressing while you count to ten, and on the count of ten to quickly get back into their lifting positions and try to lift again — it will work!

HOW TO DO A SU DOKU PUZZLE

Su doku is a type of number puzzle from Japan. The aim of the puzzle is to fill in all the missing numbers in a grid. In a su doku puzzle grid, each row has nine squares, each column has nine squares, and each box has nine squares. When the puzzle is complete, every column, row, and box must contain each of the numbers from 1 to 9 only once.

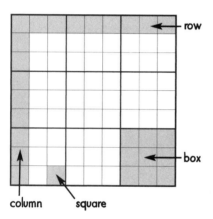

row

box

column   square

In a su doku puzzle, some numbers have already been placed in the grid. Your mission, should you accept it, is to work out the numbers that go in each of the empty squares.

Here is part of a su doku puzzle. Guess which number is missing in the top row of the grid and in the right-hand box.

You'll see that the top row contains 1, 2, 3, 4, 5, 6, 7, and 8, so the only number missing is 9. The same is true of the right-hand box.

8	4	6	2		1	3	5	7
						2		1
						6	4	8

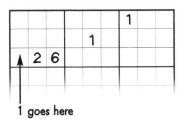

1 goes here

Solving row by row: In this example, the boxes in the middle and on the right both contain a 1. You need to work out where 1 goes in the left-hand box.

The first and second rows already contain a 1, so no other square in those rows can contain a 1. This leaves the third row. The third row in the left-hand box only has one empty square, so the missing 1 must go in there.

Solving column by column: The middle box and the right-hand box both contain a 1. To work out where the 1 goes in the left-hand box, you look at the top row. It contains a 1, so no other square in that row can contain a 1. The second row contains a 1, so no other square in that row can contain a 1. The 1 must go in the third row, but there are two empty squares in this row in the left-hand box. 1 might go in either of these squares.

1 goes here

Now, if you look down the first column you'll see that it contains a 1 already. So you know that 1 can't go in the first column of row three. The only place left is in the second column of row three.

Solving box by box:

Where in the right-hand box does the 1 go?

You can work this out by using both the columns and rows to establish in which squares the 1 can't appear.

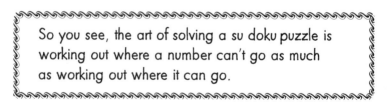

To do this, look at the left-hand box. The 1 in this box cannot be in the second row, or in the third column. That leaves two possible squares in the top row. So you know that the 1 in the left-hand box must appear in the top row.

This means that 1 cannot appear in the top row in the right-hand box. Eliminate all these squares and eliminate the ninth column because of the 1 in the fourth row. It also can't go in the middle row of the right-hand box, because the 1 appears in the middle row of the middle box.

Now you can see that there is only one square in which the 1 can go in the right-hand box.

So you see, the art of solving a su doku puzzle is working out where a number can't go as much as working out where it can go.

Now use all your new solving skills to complete the two puzzles on the following pages.

Try out your new skills on this easy puzzle.

8	9	2	5		3	6	7	4
1	5	3	6	4	7	9		8
4		6	9	2	8	1	3	5
5	3	4		6				2
	6	1		7		5	8	
7				5		4	6	9
3	8	7	1	9	5	2		6
2		9	7	8	6	3	5	1
6	1	5	2		4	8	9	7

This is the answer to the puzzle above.

8	9	2	5	1	3	6	7	4
1	5	3	6	4	7	9	2	8
4	7	6	9	2	8	1	3	5
5	3	4	8	6	9	7	1	2
9	6	1	4	7	2	5	8	3
7	2	8	3	5	1	4	6	9
3	8	7	1	9	5	2	4	6
2	4	9	7	8	6	3	5	1
6	1	5	2	3	4	8	9	7

Try out your new skills on this harder puzzle.

6			5	1	3	4	7	8
1	5	4	8	6	7	3		2
3			9		2	6	5	1
2	4	1	7					
8			1	2	4			9
					8	1	2	4
5	1	3	6		9			7
4		8	2	3	5	9	1	6
9	2	6	4	7	1			3

This is the answer to the puzzle above.

6	9	2	5	1	3	4	7	8
1	5	4	8	6	7	3	9	2
3	8	7	9	4	2	6	5	1
2	4	1	7	9	6	8	3	5
8	3	5	1	2	4	7	6	9
7	6	9	3	5	8	1	2	4
5	1	3	6	8	9	2	4	7
4	7	8	2	3	5	9	1	6
9	2	6	4	7	1	5	8	3

HOW TO FOLLOW A FRIEND WITHOUT BEING NOTICED

The key to successfully tailing a friend is to not stand out from the crowd, especially because she already knows what you look like. Wear neutral colors, such as gray or brown, and avoid clothes with distinctive patterns or logos on them. Pick clothes that are different in style from those you normally wear.

Whenever possible, walk on the opposite side of the street from the person you are following. Match your pace to theirs so you are traveling at the same speed.

Act nonchalantly. Never stare at the person you are tailing, just glance at them from time to time. If they happen to look over at you, pretend to be occupied with other things — like making calls on your cell phone or looking for a certain house.

If your target stops for any reason, you should not stop immediately. Keep on walking for a while, then stop and pretend to tie your shoelace or search in your bag for something until they start walking again.

If your target goes into a building, find a secluded spot from which you can watch the entrance until they reappear.

If your friend spots you, don't panic. Acting guilty will only give you away. Instead, act surprised to see your friend and say, "What a coincidence running into you. It really is a small world."

HOW TO MAKE A COIN DISAPPEAR

This trick needs a bit of preparation, but it's easy to perform and will amaze your audience. They will see a coin lying beside a see-through plastic cup. You will cover the cup with a handkerchief and then move the cup over the coin. When you remove the handkerchief, the coin will have vanished into thin air. Here's how it's done:

1. Take two sheets of stiff cardboard. Place the cup upside down on one sheet and draw around it. Cut out the circle.

2. Dab glue all along the rim of the cup and place the circle of cardboard on top of it. Leave it until the glue is dry. Trim off the edges of the cardboard if necessary, so that it fits exactly.

3. Put the second piece of cardboard on the table and place the plastic cup on it, upside down.

4. Ask your audience for a coin. Place it beside the cup and tell them you will make it disappear. Cover the cup with a handkerchief and move it over the top of the coin. Say "abracadabra" and remove the handkerchief. The cardboard you glued to the cup will cover the coin and make it look as if it has vanished.

5. Cover the cup again with the handkerchief and move it away from the coin — the coin will reappear.

HOW TO STUDY FOR EXAMS

Always study in a quiet place with no distractions. Some people find having music playing in the background helps them concentrate — but turn the television off.

Don't leave anything until the last minute. Well before your exams, draw up a schedule and stick to it. Make a list of the subjects you need to cover, and divide your time between them. Include breaks in your schedule for proper meals and make time to get outside for some fresh air and exercise.

Don't switch between subjects during a single study session — this will just confuse you.

Make study notes from the notes you've taken in class, but don't just copy your class notes. Make them brief and highlight key facts in different colors.

Write the facts and figures you need to memorize on flash cards that you can carry around with you. Read through them whenever you have a spare five minutes.

If you come across something you don't understand, make a note of it and ask the teacher to go over it again.

Ask one of your friends or a parent to test you on the important points after every study session.

Most important of all — don't panic about your exams. Talk to someone if you feel stressed. Remind yourself that the world will not come to an end if you fail a test. Just do your best, because your best is *the* best.

HOW TO CREATE AN OPTICAL ILLUSION

This origami project is based on an optical illusion that tricks the brain into thinking that it is seeing one complete picture rather than two different pictures in quick succession. Find a piece of cardboard about 2 x 2 inches and follow the steps below.

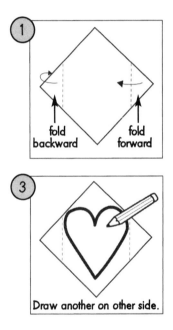

fold
backward

fold
forward

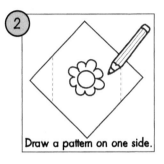

Draw a pattern on one side.

Draw another on other side.

BLOW

Hold the card between your thumb and forefinger, as shown in step four. Blow hard on one of the folded edges. The card will spin and you will see the two pictures as one.

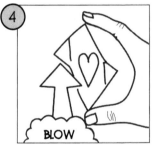

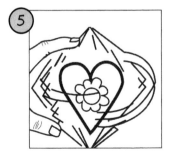

HOW TO PUT TOGETHER
THE BEST DANCE ROUTINES

It takes quite a while to memorize all the moves in a whole dance routine, so allow plenty of time to practice before your performance.

Pick a song you love and write down all the lyrics. Break the lyrics down into groups of four lines. Think of dance moves to go with each group of lines and write them down. Watch music videos for inspiration.

Start by working out the basic footwork for each move. Then add some arm and head movements.

One move should flow naturally into another, so think about how your body is positioned at the end of a move, and how to get into position for the beginning of the next move.

If you're dancing with a group of friends, make sure everyone can do the moves. Keeping it simple is better than getting it wrong.

Tip: Make sure you warm up before each practice session. Stretch out your muscles when you're finished.

HOW TO CREATE A MASTERPIECE WITH WET CHALK

Wet sticks of chalk produce ultrabright colors and you can use them on many different surfaces. If your house has a patio, why not ask if you can try creating a beautiful piece of pavement art that can be washed away easily? Skilled artists can create incredible 3-D pictures on the ground. Some can draw holes that look so real you might believe you could actually fall into them.

1. Choose the colors you want to use and place the chalk sticks upright in a glass.

2. Fill the glass with water so that about a third of the length of the chalk sticks are submerged. (If you dissolve a teaspoon of sugar in the water first, the colors will be even brighter.)

3. Leave the chalk to soak for about ten minutes. Don't leave them for too long, or the sticks will crumble.

4. Remove the chalk and lay them on a sheet of newspaper.

5. Now all you have to do is start drawing. Use the wet end of the chalk sticks. Try smudging different colors together with your fingers for an interesting effect.

6. If you are working on paper, hang your finished drawing on a clothesline to dry for a while.

HOW TO MAKE YOUR OWN LIP GLOSS

1. Put a tablespoon of petroleum jelly in a microwaveable container. Heat it on low for 30 seconds to soften it.

2. Place a teaspoon of hot water into a bowl. Add some raspberry- or strawberry-flavored powdered drink mix a tiny amount at a time, stirring constantly, until the mixture is thick.

3. Add the colored water to the petroleum jelly one drop at a time, until you get the color you want.

4. Pour your mixture into a small, clean cup and allow it to cool.

HOW TO BUILD
THE BEST SAND CASTLES

Find a good spot. You need damp sand to build with, but don't pick somewhere too close to the sea or your sand castle could get washed away. Create a firm, flat surface for your sand castle by slapping the sand with the back of a shovel and then smoothing it over.

Create the main body of your castle with buckets of sand. As you fill a bucket with sand, make sure it is tightly packed in. Tap the sides firmly and jiggle it around to get rid of any air pockets. When it's filled to the top, press it down firmly.

Build tall towers on top of your base structure by molding wet sand into pancake shapes that are as thick as your thumb and layering them on top of one another.

Squeeze handfuls of wet sand to get rid of extra moisture and stack the clumps around your castle to build a wall. Keep adding to the clumps until your wall is as high as you want. The wall should get narrower toward the top to prevent it from toppling over.

Add archways by carefully tunneling through your wall at the base and then shaping the arches using a thin stick or even a plastic knife.

As a finishing touch, dig a trench around your wall and fill it with water to make a moat for your castle.

HOW TO STRUM A GUITAR

If you can perfect the art of strumming a guitar, you'll convince the world you're a musical genius, even if you can't play a single tune. Just pick up the guitar, do an impressive couple of strums, then put it down again and say something like, "I don't really feel like playing right now," or "Too bad it's not in tune." Here's how:

Assume a rock-goddess position. If you are right-handed, hold the guitar across your body, resting it on your right knee, with the neck (the long part) pointing to your left.

Guitars have lines called frets running across the neck. These let you know where to put your fingers to play different chords. You are going to play the A chord, which involves pressing down on some of the strings between the first and second frets, right at the top of the neck.

To do this, you need to know that the string nearest your head is the bottom string and the string nearest your feet is the top string.

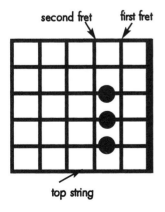

The A chord

second fret   first fret

top string

Put the ring finger of your left hand on the string that is second from the top string, then put your middle finger on the string next to that, and your index finger on the string next to that, as shown in this chord diagram.

Hold your right hand in a relaxed position over the hole in the body of the guitar. Gently brush down over the strings with your thumb. Stop there or repeat a couple of times in a confident rhythm. If you are left-handed, rest the guitar on your left knee and point the neck to your right, press the strings with your right hand, and strum with your left.

HOW TO AVOID JET LAG

If you are flying off on vacation to a place in a different time zone, prepare for your journey three days in advance.

First day: Eat a high-protein breakfast and lunch, such as bacon, eggs, sausages, or steak, and a high-carbohydrate dinner, such as pasta, potatoes, or rice.

Second day: Eat only very light meals.

Third day: Eat whatever you want.

Departure day: As soon as you get on the plane, adjust your watch to the time at your destination. Then make sure you eat meals at your normal times according to your watch. Drink plenty of water during your flight.

Stay awake during your flight if it is daytime at your destination. Sleep on the plane if it is nighttime at your destination. Use earplugs, headphones, and an eye mask to block out noise and light.

If you arrive at your destination during the day, don't go to sleep. Take a shower, then go out and do something. In the evening, eat a meal and go to bed at your normal time.

HOW TO CROSS NIAGARA FALLS
ON A TIGHTROPE

The Great Blondin was known as the greatest daredevil ever to cross Niagara Falls. He didn't just walk across the tightrope, he rode a bike, performed a backward somersault, pushed a wheelbarrow, carried his manager, and cooked an omelette halfway across.

Here's how you can gain the title "Greatest Daredevil."

First get someone you trust to set your tightrope up across the Falls. It must be really, really tight. Next make a will (just in case the stunt goes wrong) and take off your shoes and socks. Stand at one end, take a deep breath, and put your right foot diagonally across the rope with your toes pointing outward to the right. The rope will probably start to wobble, but try not to worry.

Keeping your left foot on the ground, bend your right knee and start to push down on your right foot, so that it takes most of your weight. Now lift your left foot slightly off the ground, using your arms to keep yourself balanced. Stay in that position until the rope stops wobbling, then place your left foot on the rope in front of your right foot, pointing outward to the left. Start walking.

Keep an eye out for things that might knock you off course, such as big birds or helicopters full of tourists, and mentally prepare yourself to cross the rope. The quicker you walk, the easier it will be to keep your balance, so just look straight ahead and go for it.

HOW TO EAT WITH CHOPSTICKS

1. To set up the bottom chopstick, place it between your thumb and middle finger. It should rest on the space between your thumb and index finger, as shown in the diagram here. Keep your index finger out of the way.

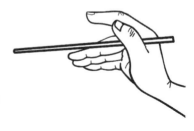

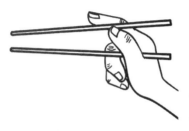

2. For the top chopstick, hold the second chopstick between your thumb and index finger, with the side of it resting against the tip of your thumb and the tip of your index finger resting on top of the chopstick.

3. The bottom chopstick should always remain still. Practice moving the top chopstick toward the bottom one. Once you have the hang of this, try picking objects up with your chopsticks until you are ready to progress to food.

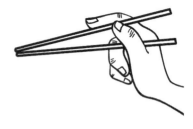

HOW TO DO A SPLIT

If you do the following stretching exercises regularly, they will help you do a split. It will take time to improve your flexibility, so don't rush things or you could injure yourself.

Warm up first by skipping with a rope or jogging in place for five minutes.

Keeping your legs and back straight, bend down from the waist and try to touch your toes. Hold this position for half a minute.

Next sit down on the ground with your legs straight out in front of you, knees together. Reach forward, bending at the waist, and try to touch your toes. Keep your back straight and try to get your chest as close to your legs as possible. Hold for half a minute.

Now kneel down and place your hands on the ground on either side of your body to support you. Stretch one leg behind you and relax. Let your body sink toward the ground. Hold for one minute and then switch legs.

After each stretching session, go into the split position and see how low you can go. As your flexibility improves, you will find you can go lower and lower. Don't strain yourself. If you feel any discomfort, stop immediately. Some people are more naturally flexible than others, so don't compare your progress to that of a friend.

Tip: Always wear loose, comfortable clothes and sneakers while performing these stretches.

HOW TO BE THE BEST AT LANGUAGES

Convince everyone you are a talented linguist by greeting people in their own language. Smile and nod knowingly while they talk to you and then take your leave in style.

Find out below how to say "hello" and "good-bye" in ten different languages.

English	"Hello"	"Good-bye"
Italian	"Ciao"	"Arrivederci"
Russian	"Privet"	"Poka"
French	"Salut"	"Au revoir"
German	"Hallo"	"Auf Wiedersehen"
Greek	"Giásou"	"Andio sas"
Japanese	"Moshi Moshi"	"Ja, mata"
Portuguese	"Ola"	"Adeus"
Spanish	"Hola"	"Adiós"
Indonesian	"Hai"	"Selamat jalon"

HOW TO SURVIVE IN THE DESERT

The most important thing to do when you find yourself alone in the desert is to find shelter from the sun. Look for shadows cast by scrub vegetation or rocks. Seek shelter during the day and travel by night, when it is much cooler.

The biggest problem you will face is the lack of water. To ensure you have a source of water, construct a "solar still."

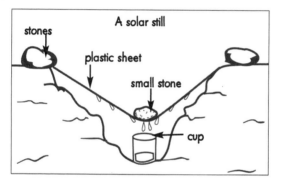

A solar still

stones

plastic sheet

small stone

cup

Take a plastic bag and cut down one side seam and along the bottom edge. Open it out so you have a large plastic sheet. Dig a shallow hole. In the middle of the hole, place a cup upright in the sand, below the level of the ground. Cover the hole with the plastic sheet and anchor it with stones around its edge. Place a small stone in the middle of the plastic so it is directly above the cup. Water vapor will condense underneath the plastic sheet and drip into the cup.

Your solar still will not provide much water, so you need to conserve as much of your bodily fluids as possible. The biggest cause of water loss is sweating. Don't cry, talk, or pant in the heat — you need to keep your mouth closed and breathe through your nose. This reduces the amount of water you lose from your body. Make sure your movements are slow and regular to keep your sweating to a minimum.

When you are hot, you will want to take off your clothes. Don't. Keep as much of your body covered as possible to protect your skin from the sun and hot winds. If you have a hat, keep it on to protect you from sunstroke and to conserve moisture. If you don't have a hat, tie a piece of cloth around your head. Make sure it hangs over the back of your neck.

Watch out for signs that you are suffering from too much heat. You will start to feel very tired and disorientated. Check the color of your urine. If it is a dark brownish yellow, you are dehydrated. The moment you are aware of any of these warning signs, drink a few sips of water. Continue to drink a little water every hour.

The large expanse of mostly empty terrain in a desert will cause you to underestimate distances. As a general rule, things are about three times farther away than you think.

Sandstorms are frequent in the desert. If you get caught in one, stay calm. Look for something to take shelter behind. Cover your nose and mouth with clothing and lie down flat, with your back to the wind, until it has passed.

HOW TO MAKE A FRENCH BRAID

French braids look great, but they can be quite tricky to do on yourself, so practice on a friend first. You need shoulder-length hair for the best results.

1. Brush the hair to get rid of any tangles, then separate a section of hair near the top of the head and divide it into three equal strands.

2. Cross the left strand over the middle strand, then do the same with the right strand, just like you would if you were doing a normal braid.

3. Now pick up some hair from directly beneath the strand that is now on the left. Add it to the left strand and cross this over the middle strand, as in step two. Repeat this with the right-hand strand.

4. Repeat this process, adding extra hair into each strand until all the loose hair has been added to the braid. Secure the end with an elastic band.

Voilà, a gorgeous French braid.

HOW TO MAKE A COMPASS

Here's one way to make a simple compass:

Pick a flat leaf and allow it to float on the surface of a cup that is full of water.

Find a sewing needle. Holding the eye of the needle, run the point down the side of a magnet. When you get to the bottom of the magnet, lift the needle off and away. Then move the point back to the top of the magnet before you stroke again. This ensures that you stroke the magnet in one direction only. Repeat at least 50 times. This has the effect of magnetizing the needle. If you don't have a magnet, you could use a silk cloth to magnetize the needle, but the effects will be much weaker.

Carefully lay the needle on the top of the leaf, and watch as the leaf slowly turns. The needle will eventually line up along the line of Earth's north and south magnetic poles, with its tip pointing north.

HOW TO FIND THE NORTH STAR

For thousands of years explorers and navigators have used the North Star (also known as Polaris) to work out their direction and latitude (their position north or south of the equator). Here's how to find the North Star in the night sky.

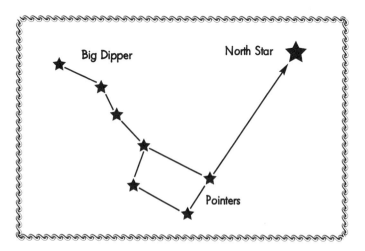

First find the Big Dipper, which is also known as the Plow. This is the constellation that looks like a saucepan (remember that depending on where you are and what time of year it is, the Big Dipper could be upside down or on its side). Once you've spotted it, locate the two stars that form the edge of the "pan" farthest away from the "handle." These stars are often called the "pointer" stars because they point to the North Star. Once you've found them, draw an imaginary line through them and this line will lead you northward to a large, bright star, which is the North Star.

HOW TO KEEP A SECRET DIARY

Don't tell anyone that you are writing a diary. If they don't know you keep one, they will not go looking for it. Frequently make comments like "Diaries are so stupid."

Disguise your diary by wrapping the jacket of another book around it. Put your camouflaged diary on a shelf with your other books.

Write "MY DIARY" on the cover of an old notebook, add a few really boring entries, and leave it lying around.

In your real diary, make up code words for people and places. Anyone who finds it will be unable to understand what you've written. Write your code down if you need to, but keep it hidden in a different place than your diary.

Write a few completely far-fetched entries like "Yesterday, I met a three-legged woman out shopping for shoes." That way, anyone who reads it will not know what is true and what is made up.

HOW TO SEND A MESSAGE IN MORSE CODE

In Morse code, each letter of the alphabet is made up of dots and dashes, the dots being short pulses and the dashes long pulses.

There are many ways you can send a message in Morse code. The easiest method is to use a flashlight. Use the Morse code alphabet below to spell out your messages.

MORSE CODE ALPHABET

A	.—	H	....	O	———	V	...—
B	—...	I	..	P	.——.	W	.——
C	—.—.	J	.———	Q	——.—	X	—..—
D	—..	K	—.—	R	.—.	Y	—.——
E	.	L	.—..	S	...	Z	——..
F	..—.	M	——	T	—		
G	——.	N	—.	U	..—		

Sit with your friend in a darkened room and transmit your message by turning the flashlight on and off. Turn the flashlight on and off quickly to represent a dot and less quickly to represent a dash. Leave the flashlight off for one second between letters and three seconds between words. Your friend will need a copy of the Morse alphabet to decipher what you are transmitting.

HOW TO PET A WILD HORSE

When attempting to deal with any animal, the best approach is to mimic its behavior. So you need to get to know exactly how horses behave so you can copy their body language.

Approach the horse from the side. A horse's eyes are on the sides of its head, so it cannot see directly in front or behind. If the horse can sense you but can't see you, it will be spooked. Move slowly and steadily at all times.

Be very calm and very cautious. Any sudden movements or loud noises may startle the horse. At best, it will run off; at worst, it might trample you.

Move toward the horse gradually, talking to it in a low, soothing voice as you do so. Don't look into the horse's eyes, as it will see this as a threat.

When you are near the horse, stop and turn sideways. This body language will be interpreted as "come here" by the horse. Continue to approach the horse in this position until you are close enough to touch it.

Reach out your hand, making sure that your fingers are pressed together and not spread out. Gently stroke the horse's neck.

HOW TO SURVIVE AN ALIEN INVASION

Aliens usually invade large cities where they can cause maximum death and destruction, so when news of an invasion first breaks, consider moving to the countryside.

Alien spaceships are very large and hard to miss. This gives you an advantage. If, in the middle of the day, the sun is suddenly blocked out and there is no eclipse scheduled in your area, take immediate action and alert the authorities.

Stockpile enough food and water to keep your family alive for several weeks and barricade yourself in your house. Aliens are supremely intelligent beings, but they often have trouble with simple things such as doorknobs, or going up and down stairs. So hide in the largest upstairs room in your house. Aliens are also easily confused by their own reflection, so line the room with every mirror you can find in the house.

Alien spacecraft often have a disastrous effect on electrical circuits, so don't rely on your parents' car to get away. Make sure your bike has plenty of air in the tires in case you need to use it in an emergency.

Aliens will sometimes try to disguise themselves as humans. Luckily they are not very good at it. If you come across an incredibly short man with glowing red eyes and a strange, echoing voice, trust your instincts and run away as fast as you can.

Alien races often have fatal reactions to things that are commonplace on Earth, such as water or the cold virus. If you come face-to-face with a creature from another planet, try squirting it with a water pistol or sneezing on it.

HOW TO FINGER KNIT

Finger knitting uses the same techniques as knitting with needles. Try finger knitting first, then move on to using needles when you feel more confident. Use the following finger-knitting method to make a long strip of knitting to wear as a headband.

1. Get a ball of yarn. Wrap the end of the yarn loosely around the index finger of your left hand (or right hand if you are left-handed) and tie a knot in it. The loose end 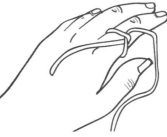 of the yarn should be hanging down the back of your hand.

2. Weave the working end of the yarn (the bit attached to the ball) behind your middle finger, in front of your ring finger, and then behind your little finger. Make sure the loops are not too tight.

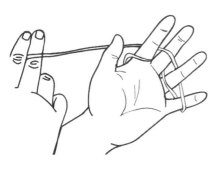

3. Now weave back to your index finger, so the yarn goes in front of your little finger, behind the ring finger, and so on. Then repeat steps two and three, so you have two strands of yarn on each finger. The second weave of yarn should lie above the first weave.

4. Starting at your little finger, lift the bottom loop of yarn over the top loop. Slip it off your finger and drop it behind your hand. Repeat with the bottom loop on your ring finger. Continue in this way until all four fingers

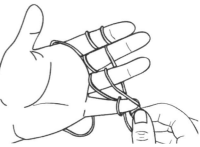

have only one strand of yarn wrapped around them.

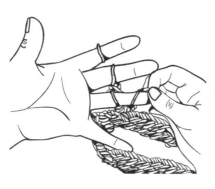

5. Start weaving, so you have two strands around each finger. Then repeat step four. Keep going until you have a knitted strip behind your hand long enough to go around your head if you are making a knitted headband.

6. To finish, make sure you are at a point where there is only one strand of yarn on each finger. Lift the loop off your little finger. Slip it onto your ring finger, so that this finger holds two strands of yarn. Lift the bottom strand on your ring finger over the top one and slip it off your finger. Drop it behind your hand. Lift the remaining loop off your ring finger and slip it onto your middle finger. Repeat until you are left with one strand on your index finger. Cut the yarn off the ball, leaving a 6-inch tail. Feed the tail through the remaining loop. Slip it off your finger and pull it tight to secure the end of your knitting.

HOW TO BE THE BEST AT TEXT MESSAGING

The world record for the fastest texting is constantly being broken. It currently stands at 160 characters in 41.52 seconds. Now that won't be easy to beat, but the best way to speed up your messages per minute is to use text abbreviations. Here are some useful ones:

(((H)))	hugs
AML	all my love
ASAP	as soon as possible
B4	before
B4N	bye for now
BBL	be back later
BF	best friend
CUL8R	see you later
FOMCL	falling off my chair laughing
FYEO	for your eyes only
G2G	got to go
GB	good-bye
GL	good luck
GR8	great

HAND	have a nice day
HRU?	how are you?
IC	I see
IDK	I don't know
ILBL8	I will be late
IMO	in my opinion
JK	just kidding
KOTC	kiss on the cheek
LOL	laughing out loud
NBD	no big deal
NE1	anyone
OTB	off to bed
OTOH	on the other hand
PCM	please call me
PU!	that stinks!
RUOK?	are you OK?
SRY	sorry
THX	thanks
TMB	text me back
WKD	weekend
X	kiss

HOW TO PERSUADE YOUR PARENTS TO GET A PET

Before you start your pet-purchase campaign, be sure that you really do want a pet and are prepared to take full responsibility for it.

Think carefully about the kind of animal your household can accommodate and look after. You might be dying to own a pony, but if you live in a city it is probably not a great idea.

Research as much as you can about the animal of your choice. The more knowledge you have, the easier it will be to convince your parents that you have really put some genuine thought into it.

Before approaching your parents, make a list of all the possible objections they may have. Try to come up with reasonable answers to all of their concerns.

Be persistent with your request, but always remain calm and polite. Tantrums and tears will only prove that you are not mature enough to look after a pet.

Consider getting an after-school job that involves looking after animals. You could try dog-walking, helping out at your local stable, or volunteering at an animal shelter. This will help your parents feel more confident about your ability to care for your proposed pet.

If you have a friend who owns the kind of animal you want, invite her over to talk pet care with your parents.

Start off by thinking small. If your parents are adamant that you can't have that puppy you long for, ask them to consider letting you have a smaller animal, such as a hamster or a goldfish. If you take good care of the small animal over a long period of time, they may reconsider buying you the puppy you really wanted. Alternatively, you may discover you and your fishy friend are completely happy.

HOW TO WIN A BET

Make a bet with your friends that they cannot fold a piece of paper in half more than seven times. It sounds easy, but no matter how big the piece of paper, it is impossible to do. Feel free to promise your friends anything if they succeed. Don't worry — they won't be able to.

HOW TO MAKE A BASKET

The moment the basketball is passed to you, turn and line up your body with the hoop. Check that your feet, shoulders, and elbows are square with the basket. Make sure your feet are planted shoulder-width apart to increase your balance.

Take a deep breath, steady yourself, and focus on the back of the rim. Don't allow the defenders to break your concentration.

Balance the ball on the tips of the fingers of your right hand (the left hand if you are left-handed). Place your other hand on the side of the ball to keep it steady.

Stretch your arms above your head so that the ball is aimed at the hoop.

When you are ready to shoot (and don't let anyone rush you), bend your knees and squat, keeping your back straight and your eyes on the basket.

Move your hands back slightly behind your head. As you jump up, move your hands forward and upward. Straighten your arms. As you straighten them, release the ball toward the hoop.

To improve your chances of scoring, spin the ball backward as you release it by flicking your wrists. This way, if the ball bounces on the rim it is more likely to go in.

HOW TO READ BODY LANGUAGE

Sometimes someone will tell you one thing, but their body language will be "suggesting" something completely different. Use the list below to figure out how people are really feeling.

Biting nails: anxiety, insecurity

Lounging on chair with arms dangling: relaxed

Clenched jaw, tense muscles: anger

Arms crossed: defensiveness

Hands clasped behind head: confidence

Touching or rubbing nose: rejection, lying

Looking down, face turned away: disbelief

Tapping or drumming fingers: impatience

Patting hair: insecurity

Tilted head: interest

Stroking chin: making a decision

Pulling at ear: indecision

Pinching bridge of nose, eyes closed: apprehension

HOW TO GROW A CRYSTAL

1. Make a saturated salt solution by dissolving normal table salt in warm water. You will know when the solution is saturated, because no more salt will dissolve and you'll see grains of salt at the bottom of the container.

2. Pour the solution into a clean jar, filling it about a third full. Keep the rest of the solution handy.

3. Use a length of string to tie a small, clean pebble to a pencil. Suspend the pebble in the salt water with the pencil over the mouth of the jar. The pebble should not touch the bottom of the jar.

4. Leave your jar somewhere warm, such as on a sunny windowsill. Allow the water to evaporate. Check it every few days and fill up the jar with the rest of the salt solution as necessary to keep the pebble covered.

5. As the salt solution evaporates, crystals will begin to form on the pebble. After a few weeks, you should have a lovely crystal.

To create a colored crystal, you should add a few drops of food coloring to the salt solution.

HOW TO MAKE YOUR OWN BREAD

Making your own bread involves a lot of strenuous kneading, but it will taste much better than prepackaged loaves and it smells delicious when baking in the oven. Plus, if you do it often, you will develop seriously buff arms.

1. Put 8 ounces (or about 2 cups) of plain flour in a mixing bowl and add 1 teaspoon of salt and 1 teaspoon of sugar.

2. Add 1 tablespoon of soft margarine or butter and mix it into the flour with your fingers.

3. Add 1 packet of dry yeast to the bowl and mix it in thoroughly, again using your fingers.

4. Add a ½ cup of warm water to the bowl. Make sure the water is warm but not too hot, or your bread won't rise.

5. Stir the mixture with a wooden spoon until it starts to thicken. When it gets too hard to use the spoon, wash your hands thoroughly, and use them to knead the dough until it starts coming away from the sides of the bowl, leaving them clean.

6. Now comes the hard work. Sprinkle flour over a flat work surface and place the dough on it. You need to knead the dough until it is smooth and stretchy. Use the heel of your hand to push the dough away from you, then squash it back into a ball with your knuckles, turn it over and repeat. Keep doing this for about five minutes.

7. Lightly brush the dough with vegetable oil. Wrap a clean dish towel around it and put it somewhere warm, like your kitchen counter. The warmth will activate the yeast, which will, in turn, make the dough rise and swell.

8. When it has doubled in size, punch your dough to knock the air out of it — this is called "knocking back" the dough. Then shape the dough into the form you want your loaf to take.

9. Your dough is now ready to bake. Preheat the oven to 450°F.

10. Remove the dish towel and place the dough on a greased baking tray. Bake it in the oven for about 25 minutes. The loaf is done when it turns golden brown and you can hear a hollow sound when you tap the underside.

11. Place your loaf on a wire rack to cool so that it doesn't get soggy. Eat it as soon as it is cool for a taste of yeasty-fresh, oven-baked heaven.

HOW TO BE A PRIMA BALLERINA

Becoming a prima ballerina takes hard work, dedication, and regular lessons. To get you started, practice these basic positions.

Always keep your weight balanced evenly on both legs and make sure that your back is straight and that you are facing straight ahead.

First position: Turn your feet out to the sides so that they form a straight line. Your heels should be touching. Make sure you are turning your whole leg out from the hip, not just your foot. Hold your hands out in front of you at waist level, so that they form an oval shape (imagine you are holding a beach ball in front of you).

Second position: Your feet should be placed as in first position, but spaced a foot's length apart.

Stretch your arms out to the sides, angled slightly downward, with your palms facing downward.

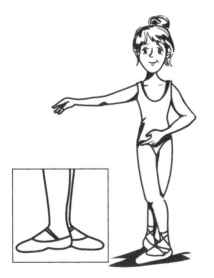

Third position: With your toes still pointing out to the sides as in the first two positions, cross one foot halfway in front of the other, so that the heel is level with the arch of the back foot.

One arm should be in first position (held out in front of you) and the other should be in second position (out to the side).

112

Fourth position: This position is a little harder. With your toes still pointing out to the sides, bring one foot in front of the other with your toes and heels in line with each other. Make sure there is a space the length of one of your feet between the front and back foot.

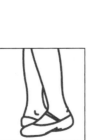

One arm should be in second position and the other should be brought up in a curve above your head.

Fifth position: This is the hardest position of them all. Place one foot exactly in front of the other, as in the fourth position, but they should be touching each other.

Bring both arms up in a curve so that they are above and slightly in front of your head.

HOW TO MAKE A PAPIER-MÂCHÉ BOWL

1. To make papier-mâché paste, pour ½ a cup of plain flour into a saucepan containing 2 cups of cold water. Put your pan on the burner of your stove and add 2 cups of boiling water. Bring to a boil while stirring constantly. Take the pan off the heat, stir in 3 tablespoons of sugar, and allow the paste to cool.

2. Cover the area you are going to work on with newspaper, as this is a very messy project.

3. A balloon makes an excellent mold for a bowl. So blow up a balloon and tie it shut at the neck.

4. Tear off narrow strips of newspaper about 8 inches long and dip them into the paste. Run your fingers down the strips to get rid of any excess paste and then drape them over your balloon. Smooth the strips down to get rid of any lumps and bumps. Repeat this until the bottom half of the balloon is covered (leave the neck half clear).

5. Allow this layer of strips to dry before you add another layer on top. Add several layers of paper and paste to the balloon, letting each layer dry first.

6. When the newspaper has dried completely, you can pop the balloon and peel it away from the newspaper.

7. Use a pair of scissors to cut a smooth edge for your bowl. Then decorate it with paint and glitter.

HOW TO LOOK AFTER BABY CHICKS

Find a cage that is large enough for the chicks. Each one will need at least 16 square inches of space. Cover the bottom of the cage with 1 inch of wood shavings.

Chicks need to be kept warm. You will need a special 250-watt lightbulb. The lightbulb should be about 18 inches above the bottom of the cage.

Make sure that part of the cage is sheltered from the heat of the bulb, so the chicks can move there if they get too hot. Keep drafts out by covering the outside of the cage with cardboard.

Teach the chicks where to go for food by sprinkling some of their feed underneath the feeder.

Frequently check that the chicks have enough water. Gently dip each chick's beak into the water when you place it in the cage to let them know it is there.

HOW TO TELL WHAT SOMEONE IS LIKE FROM THEIR HANDWRITING

Analyzing someone's handwriting can reveal secrets about their personality. Get your friends to give you samples of their handwriting and look out for some of the following characteristics:

What lovely neat writing

Very neat writing means the person is reliable and good at communicating with others. Sloppy writing indicates the person is secretive.

Larger than life

Small and shy

Large letters point to someone who likes to be the center of attention. Small letters mean the person is shy and has a good eye for detail.

Sloping left   *Sloping right*

If the handwriting slopes to the left, the person is good at keeping their feelings to themselves. If it slopes to the right, they are open and honest.

Every letter separate

Flowing and joined up

Writing that isn't joined up shows that the person is artistic. Joined-up writing points to someone who is very cautious.

Spiky letters

Rounded letters

Rounded letters means the person is logical and usually gets things right. Spiky letters point to someone who is quick-thinking and perceptive.

HOW TO COPE IF ZOMBIES ATTACK

Zombies are known as the "living dead" because they are dead people whose bodies have been mysteriously revived. It is fairly easy to spot zombies because, although they look a lot like normal people, their flesh is a rotten green color because they are decaying. They tend to stumble around as if dazed, moaning and groaning. The terrifying thing about zombies, however, is that they will pursue you relentlessly and are hard to stop.

If you hear on the TV or radio news of a zombie invasion, you need to act fast. Zombies multiply very quickly. If a zombie bites or scratches someone, their victim will soon mutate into a zombie, too. Sadly, there is no cure — once a zombie, always a zombie. So it is essential to get to safety as quickly as possible.

Choose a secure place to hide out. First check the news broadcasts regularly to find out which areas are zombie hot spots and which are less dangerous. You'll need plenty of food and water. A supermarket makes an ideal base.

Lock all doors and windows, and pile heavy objects against them for extra security. However, make sure you have an emergency exit if zombies do get into the building.

If you need to venture out for supplies, dress in bite-proof clothing at all times. Full biker's leathers are perfect. Failing that, go for lots of layers.

If you find yourself in the middle of a crowd of walking dead, pretend to be one of them. Tilt your head to one side, drool, and moan. Hold your arms out in front of you and stare straight ahead. Try to limp slowly right through the pack. If they spot you, run for it. Zombies are slow-moving and stupid. If you change directions frequently, create diversions (such as overturning chairs), and scream — it will completely confuse them.

Don't waste your energy fighting, because zombies are hard to kill (mainly because they are already dead). You can destroy them by cutting off their heads or crushing their brains. Some zombies will die if you burn their bodies, but individual body parts have been known to keep moving even after they have been cut off.

If you have no choice but to stand and fight a zombie, always check your body carefully for bite marks afterward.

Also Available:
THE BOYS' BOOK: HOW TO BE THE BEST AT EVERYTHING

At last, the perfect guide for boys who want to know how to do…everything! Ever wonder how to:

- Fight off a crocodile?
- Rip a phonebook in half?
- Make a boomerang?
- Escape quicksand?
- Speak in code?
- Read your friends' minds?
- Make a waterbomb?

Well, you're in luck! Inside you'll find out how to do all of these amazing things—and much, much more!